THE
MYSTERY
OF...

STONEHENGE

BY
HARRIETTE ABELS

EDITED BY
Dr. Howard Schroeder
Professor in Reading and Language Arts
Dept. of Curriculum and Instruction
Mankato State University

PUBLISHED BY
CRESTWOOD HOUSE

CIP

LIBRARY OF CONGRESS CATALOGING IN PUBLICATION DATA

Abels, Harriette Sheffer.
Stonehenge.

(The Mystery of ——)
SUMMARY: Examines the various mysteries of the ancient megalithic monument Stonehenge, discussing the possibilities regarding who built it, how they constructed it, and what its purpose was.
1. Stonehenge (England)—Juvenile literature. 2. Megalithic monuments—England—Wiltshire—Juvenile literature. 3. England—Antiquities—Juvenile literature. 4. Wiltshire—Antiquities—Juvenile literature. [1. Stonehenge (England) 2. Megalithic monuments. 3. England—Antiquities] I. Title. II. Series.
DA142.A24   1987   936.2'319   87-13638
ISBN 0-89686-346-8

International Standard
Book Number:
0-89686-346-8

Library of Congress
Catalog Card Number:
87-13638

CREDITS

Illustrations:
Cover Photo: Peter R. Hornby
Dr. Gerald S. Hawkins: 4-5, 8, 10-11, 13, 14, 18-19, 28-29, 30-31, 34-35, 40-41, 42-43
Peter R. Hornby: 7, 44-45
Bob Williams: 16, 21, 22, 24-25, 27
AP/Wide World Photos: 32
Mark E. Ahlstrom: 37, 38-39
Andy Schlabach: 46
Graphic Design & Production:
Baker Street Productions, Ltd.

CRESTWOOD HOUSE

Box 3427, Mankato, MN, U.S.A. 56002

STONEHENGE

TABLE OF CONTENTS

The giant stones of Stonehenge can be eerie when viewed in the moonlight.

Chapter 1

Giant stones loom in the shadows of moonlight. Eerie figures dressed in long robes sway in the dim light. The sound of ancient chants fills the air. The Druids are celebrating Midsummer's Eve. Their ceremonies date back to ancient times—but not as ancient as the ghostly stones that tower over them.

This is Stonehenge. Stonehenge is the oldest pre-historic structure in western Europe. It stands on a vast open clearing called Salisbury Plain in southwest England. Every year thousands of people come to see this ancient pattern of stone.

When you first see it, Stonehenge looks like a jumbled pile of very large rocks. Some stand straight and tall. Others are tipped or leaning. Still others lie flat on the ground.

There are many unanswered questions about Stonehenge. We aren't sure <u>who</u> built it. We aren't sure <u>why</u>

it was built. We aren't sure how it was built. We aren't even sure what it is. But many archaeologists (scientists who study the remains of past human life) have made intelligent guesses.

Stonehenge is built in the shape of a circle. Why? What was it used for? Archaeologists think they know when Stonehenge was built. They are fairly sure they know how it was done. But they don't know its real purpose. One reason is because there are no written records from that time. Writing was not used in England until the country was conquered by the Romans. That happened about fifteen hundred years after Stonehenge was built.

Many scientists agree that Stonehenge was some form of religious temple, but it is not known what gods were worshipped by the people of this area. Nor do we know what types of ceremonies may have taken place there.

For many years, scientists thought that the temple was connected to sun worshippers. On the longest day of the year (June 21st) the sun rises directly over the peak of the Heel Stone. On the shortest day of the year (December 21st) the sun sets exactly opposite the Heel Stone, its rays shining through the old entrance-way. This has led some archaeologists to believe that Stonehenge was built to celebrate some great festival in the winter of the year.

Other scientists think that the full moon had something to do with the ancient worship. The tip of the earth's axis has changed slightly since Stonehenge was built. The midsummer sun would have been farther left

For many years experts thought that Stonehenge was built by people who worshipped the sun.

(north) at that time, and so the sun's rays would have been over the top of the Heel Stone.

In 1963, an astrophysicist named Gerald Hawkins suggested that Stonehenge might possibly have been a very accurate astronomical calendar. Dr. Hawkins drew imaginary lines connecting the stones at Stonehenge. Aided by a modern computer, Hawkins found the imaginary lines to be remarkably accurate. They were exactly right for predicting the rising and setting of the

7

sun and the moon around the year 1500 B.C. Whoever built Stonehenge seems to have had a vast knowledge of astronomy. The chances of anyone putting the stones in exactly the right place by accident is about one in a hundred million.

It was through Dr. Hawkins' work that scientists began to suspect that the builders of the Stonehenge observatory may have been following the moon, and not the sun. The pattern of the moonrise is more involved than that of the sun. The moon pattern has to be watched over a period of about nineteen years before it can be accurately seen. This means that the people of Stonehenge were even more scientifically advanced than was earlier thought.

Today, we still have no definite answer to our questions. Was Stonehenge merely a religious temple? Was it a calendar of the seasons? Or was it a precise astronomical observatory, built by people whose scientific knowledge was almost as exact as the knowledge we have today?

Dr. Gerald Hawkins was the first expert to suggest that the stones at Stonehenge may be an astronomical calendar.

Chapter 2

John Aubrey was an English archaeologist who lived in the seventeenth century. In those days, he was called an antiquary, meaning "someone who studies ancient things." Around the year 1660 A.D., he wrote the first detailed account of the strange stone monument on Salisbury Plain. Since that time, Stonehenge has been thoroughly studied.

The scientists working at Stonehenge today are called astro-archaeologists. It is only recently that astro-archaeology has been accepted as a professional science. In the last twenty years, modern scientific methods have brought us much closer to solving the riddle of Stonehenge.

The Stonehenge we see today is really the result of three separate building stages. They are called Stone-henge I, Stonehenge II, and Stonehenge III. Scientists know now how it must have looked at all three stages. They have drawn sketches of how each stage probably looked, and have even lifted some of the fallen stones back into their original places.

Stonehenge I was built during the Stone Age, about 2200 B.C. At that time, it was a simple, open-air temple. There was a large circular space nearly one

The Heel Stone is the only stone left from Stonehenge I.

hundred yards (91 m) across, which was enclosed by
a dirt bank (embankment) and a deep ditch. There was
an entrance to the circle on the northeast side. Outside
there was an archway made of wood. The only stone
left from this period is still standing. It is now called
the Heel or Sun Stone.

There was also a ring of fifty-six pits, three feet (1 m)

deep. They are known as the Aubrey Holes, named after John Aubrey. We do not know what the holes were used for. We do know that they were simply holes; they were not made to hold stones or wooden posts. Some archaeologists think the Aubrey Holes may have had some religious meaning. Many years later, these holes were used for the burial of human bones.

11

The second stage of Stonehenge probably was built between 1700 and 1600 B.C. A tribe called the Beaker people had spread across eastern and southern England several hundred years earlier. It is thought that they came across the North Sea from somewhere on the European continent. These people took down Stonehenge's two entrance stones and the wooden archway. They dug a narrow ditch around the Heel Stone, then filled it up again, perhaps as part of a magical protection ritual. They also built a long avenue connecting Stonehenge to the river Avon.

Now the real work began. A number of bluestones, called that because of their color, were brought from southwest Wales, about 140 miles (225 km) away. They were set up in two circles inside the original circle. These stones are roughly shaped as flat slabs and tall columns.

For some reason, this arrangement of two circles was never finished. There is evidence that at least half of the stones were put up. There are still traces of the holes where they stood. But something changed the minds of the builders, and they took down the stones that had already been put in place.

The third stage of Stonehenge dates from about 1600 B.C. This was the beginning of the Bronze Age. Across the Irish Sea, in Ireland, people were making tools and weapons of bronze. They were also beginning to make ornaments of gold. These goods were traded, not only in England and Scotland, but also in Europe. This is probably where the tribes living near Stonehenge got the wealth needed to build the remarkable stone temple. This version of Stonehenge was built with Sarsen stones, a type of natural sandstone. The stones were brought from Marlborough Downs, about twenty miles (32 km) away.

This time the arrangement of stones was much more complex. We cannot be sure how it was actually done, but scientists have developed a very logical theory. The first stones to be raised must have been the upright ones of the inner horseshoe arrangement. They are the heaviest and the tallest. Through their diggings,

The stones of the inner horseshoe are the heaviest and tallest.

13

scientists feel that some of these stones were pulled up into place from their outer side. This could have been done only if the workers had a wide open space in which to work. There is an outer circle of stones around the horseshoe that must have been put up last, otherwise those stones would have been in the way of building the inner horseshoe.

The Altar Stone is now mostly covered by this fallen lintel.

14

Near the center of the inner circle is the Altar Stone. It comes from the same area as the bluestones. But it is the only stone in the temple of this particular type.

This stage of Stonehenge was a long time in the making. It probably took several hundred years, and it was never totally finished.

There are also signs that the design of the temple was changed several times while it was being built. The last stages of work were probably finished around 1300 B.C.

It is not known whether Stonehenge was originally the idea of one person or of a group of people. We do know that it took many people hundreds of years of hard labor to build the three stages of Stonehenge. Along the way, they left valuable clues to help modern scientists figure out who they were and why they undertook this enormous task.

Chapter 3

Who built Stonehenge and why did they build it? We probably will never know for sure. For many years the temple's builders were thought to be the Druids. They were the judges and priests of a people called the Celts.

The Celts were an ancient tribe that came to the British Isles from middle Europe around 500 B.C. Much

For many years it was thought that the Druids built Stonehenge. This drawing shows what it may have looked like when it was finished.

of their worship centered around the seasons of the year. The Druids (judges and priests) held mystic ceremonies at Stonehenge. There are ancient tales of ghostly figures dancing in the moonlight around the grey stone columns. Even today, modern Druids come to Stonehenge to watch the midsummer sunrise.

But we know that the original Druids came much later in English history than the stone builders—almost one thousand years later! Stonehenge must have already been an eerie ruin when they arrived. And we know that the Celts did not have the technical or engineering knowledge needed to build this remarkable structure.

This brings up the most puzzling question of all: Where did the people who first dreamed of Stonehenge get the knowledge and inspiration to build it? There are other stone clusters scattered throughout the British Isles and western Europe. None of those structures show the brilliant mathematical and engineering knowledge that was needed to build Stonehenge.

In 1953, archaeologists discovered some carved symbols on the Sarsen stones. Most of these symbols are pictures of bronze axe-heads. They look like the tools made in England about 1600 B.C. The markings can only be seen when the sun shines on them in a certain way; they were discovered by pure luck. There are several dozen of these axe-head designs. There also are other symbols that are too faint to identify.

One theory is that the axe-head drawings are connected to the axe cult in ancient Greece. They may have

An ancient carved dagger is seen on one of the Sarsen stones.

been cut into the rock as token gifts to the temple.

There is also a carving of a dagger. It seems to be the same as the daggers used in Greece at that time. In the area around Stonehenge, in many of the barrows (burial holes), beads and other ornaments have been found. They have been traced back to countries around the Mediterranean Sea. It also is known that trading went on between England and Germany and other middle European countries at that time. If the dagger

seen on the Sarsen stone is Greek, it may answer the question of Stonehenge's designer. Perhaps it was someone who had been on one of those trading expeditions. Or maybe the designer was Greek and was familiar with prehistoric Greek buildings.

Civilization was much more advanced in Greece and the Middle Eastern countries at that time. There is a theory that the designer of Stonehenge may have been trained as a mathematician or as an architect. Even though many daily activities in those countries were tied to religious beliefs, a number of the basic sciences were understood.

The people who lived in this part of England during the time Stonehenge was built used a crude form of agriculture. It was called digging-stick culture, and was practiced exactly as it sounds. Small holes were dug in the ground with sharp sticks; into these, seeds were planted. These people also raised their own domestic animals, such as cattle, pigs, sheep, and dogs. Crude mining of flint was done in local mines. But nowhere is there any evidence that these local people had the knowledge to build Stonehenge.

In John Aubrey's time, some writers attributed Stonehenge to Merlin, the wizard of King Arthur's court. Others gave credit to a people they called "the stonemovers." Even today, modern writers weave their own favorite theories into fiction stories.

Stonehenge is a puzzle that has intrigued every generation for hundreds of years. Because the local people of 2200-1600 B.C. had no written language, they were unable to leave us a written record of their history, as was done in other parts of the world, such as Greece and Egypt.

One recent theory holds that the people were indeed stonemovers. Perhaps the work of the men of the tribe consisted only of moving the gigantic stones, and erecting them into the pre-planned form of the temple. The knowledge of how to do this difficult work would have been passed on from father to son.

Why was Stonehenge abandoned before it was completely finished? We know it had been worked on for hundreds of years. Perhaps the local people were unable to protect themselves against invading tribes from the north. Or maybe, as the people became more civilized, they became interested in other things. There may have come a time when a generation of the tribe finally realized that they no longer remembered why they buried their dead in this mystical circle. Maybe they no longer remembered who had told their ancestors to spend their lives smoothing and setting up the giant stones. Maybe they decided they had better things to do.

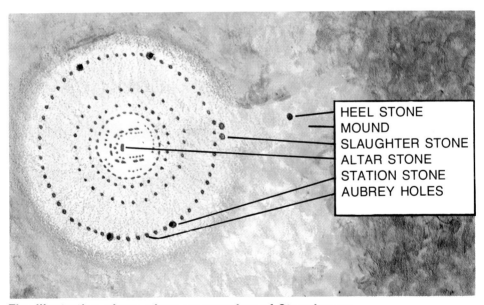

HEEL STONE
MOUND
SLAUGHTER STONE
ALTAR STONE
STATION STONE
AUBREY HOLES

The illustration above gives an overview of Stonehenge.

21

Chapter 4

For centuries, the greatest mystery about Stonehenge was how it was built. Some of the methods used for building have been discovered during the study of the site. We know that the ditches and pits, and the holes for the stones, were dug with pickaxes made from the antlers of deer. The shovels were made from the

Deer antlers and shoulder blades of cattle were used to dig the holes for the stones.

shoulder blades of cattle. The debris left over was shoveled into baskets. Modern archaeologists have tried using these simple tools to prove that it could be done. To their surprise, the tools worked almost as well as our modern picks, shovels, and buckets.

Scientists have always known that the stones used to build Stonehenge did not come from Salisbury Plain. But the big mystery is how these mammoth stones were brought to the site.

Modern scientists can tell where the stones came from by looking at pieces of them under a microscope. The bluestones of the inner circle came from mountains in Pembrokeshire in south Wales. This is 140 miles (225 km) away from Stonehenge.

It is thought that the stones were put on boats and rafts and brought by water. This would have been much easier than dragging them over the land. The builders would have been able to choose from thousands of boulders of all shapes and sizes lying on the ground in the mountains. Such stones still lie there today. The stones then would have been loaded onto a type of large sled and taken down to the shore. There they would have been put onto rafts. The wind and the tide would have taken the raft along the south coast of Wales to the mouth of the river Avon. There the stones would have been put into boats that were made by hollowing out tree trunks. Several of these ''canoes'' would have been lashed side by side, with a deck on top to hold the stones. This type of boat would float, even with its

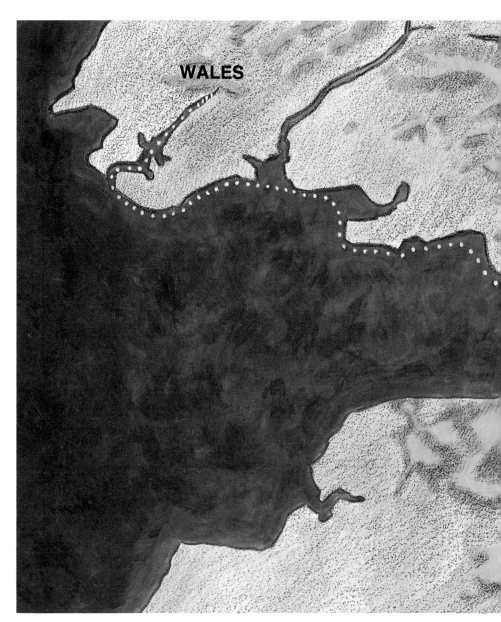

Shown above is the probable route of the bluestones from the mountains on the coast of Wales to Salisbury Plain. On the river Avon,
the stones could have been carried on several "canoes" that were
lashed together.

24

SALISBURY
PLAIN

Avon
River

Stonehenge

heavy load, in the shallow rivers. The rafts were safer at sea because they could not sink, but on the rivers, they might possibly run aground. Once the stones were back on land, they would have been put on the low sleds again, and dragged onto Salisbury Plain.

Some scientists have suggested that the bluestones may have been brought to the Salisbury area many years earlier. There may have been an older temple built entirely of the bluestones. The scientists do not think that this earlier temple was on the same site as Stonehenge; however, it is possible that the same bluestones were used in both places.

The Sarsen stones, which form the outer circle, come from the Wiltshire district. This is only about twenty miles (32 km) away from Stonehenge. Like the bluestones, the Sarsen stones were also picked up from the ground. Many thousands of these stones can still be found at Wiltshire. Some of the heaviest Sarsens weigh about fifty tons (45 MT). These stones would have been dragged over land, as there are no rivers large enough to float them on. These giant stones were dragged through thick forests, where new paths had to be cut, and up steep slopes leading to Salisbury Plain. It has been estimated that to pull the heaviest stone up that hill would have taken at least a thousand men.

Once the stones arrived at the site, they had to be put in place. Today, we would just drive a huge crane onto the plain and let the machine do the work. But a thousand years ago, the only power was manpower.

In the past, there were many theories as to how this was done. The process of erecting the stones in Stonehenge probably went something like this: A huge hole was dug in the chalky ground. One side of the hole was sloping. The other side was protected with stakes to keep it straight. The stone was pulled up to the hole on rollers. That way it could be balanced like a seesaw on the front roller. The top of the stone was then lifted with levers so the bottom slipped into the hole, resting against the sloping side. A layer of logs was pushed bencath the stone to brace it. The top was then raised a few inches, with the levers resting on the piled logs. Each time the stone was raised, more logs were quickly shoved under it to brace it up. Finally, ropes made of cow hide, or strips of leather, were tied around the top of the stone. Then many men would pull it the rest of the way

With levers and layered logs, the stones were set into holes. Then many men, using ropes, could pull the stones upright.

27

Stonehenge is made up of natural stone and "dressed" stone. The stones in the circle (left) are mostly natural, while the stones in the horseshoe (right) have been dressed, or shaped by hand.

upright. The bottom of the stone would settle into the chalky bed.

Stonehenge is made up of natural stone and dressed

stone. Natural stones have not been smoothed or shaped. Dressed stones are the result of long and hard work. They were pounded with hammers made of heavy stone. This gradually smoothed away the natural rough surface.

A horizontal stone, called a lintel, connected most of the Sarsen stones. A tenon, used to hold the lintel in place, can be seen on the top of the stone in the center of the picture.

The stones that were used had been lying on the ground for thousands of years. They were rough and pitted from blowing dirt and sand. Their edges were worn down by wind, rain, and snow. The stones that were used are very hard. Even today, it is difficult to cut them with modern steel tools.

Some of the stone hammers used in the dressing were as big as a football. The dressing must have been done while the giant stones were still lying flat on the ground.

30

After they were raised into place, the stone hammers were wedged into the holes to act as supports.

The bluestones were arranged in a circle and a horseshoe. Many of the stones are now missing. The stones that make up the circle are mostly natural ones. Those in the horseshoe have been carefully dressed.

Many of the Sarsen stones are connected by a lintel. This is a square stone lying across the tops of the other stones. The lintel is held tightly by a tenon and mortise.

This photo, taken in 1944, shows how carefully some of the lintels were fitted to the stones.

The tenon is a small lump sticking up from the top of the upright stones, made by dressing the top of the stone. Someone would climb to the top and level it by pounding and chipping the rock away, leaving the tenon sticking up in the air. Meanwhile, the lintel was shaped into a rectangle while it was still on the ground. In the bottom of the lintel, a rectangular hole (the mortise) was hollowed out to fit the tenon that had been left on the top of the erect stone.

In order to get the lintel on top of the stones, a huge platform would be built, one level at a time, out of stacked timber. The platform surrounded the two stones on which the lintel was going to be placed. The platform probably was built a foot or two at a time as the lintel was levered onto the next level, until finally the top of the uprights was reached. Then the lintel could be settled onto the stones, the tenon and mortise holding the heavy top stone firmly in place.

The word Henge means 'a hanging' or 'a gallows cross.' It was probably used at Stonehenge to mean 'a stone doorway.' With the lintels set in place on top of the upright stones, the openings between do look like doorways.

Archaeologists believe that the key to Stonehenge is the Heel Stone. It is the only upright stone that stands outside the circle. All of the accurate astronomical measurements begin with the Heel Stone. It seems as if the rest of Stonehenge was built with the Heel Stone as the central point.

The sun rises over the Heel Stone on the longest day of the year—
June 21st.

34

Chapter 5

There are hundreds of old legends about Stonehenge. Today, although we may not be sure what it was, we do know what it wasn't! These are some of the guesses made by writers, artists, and scientists of the past.

Ancient writers thought it was a king's palace or a royal sports arena. One story says that the wizard, Merlin, told King Arthur the stones had healing powers. There were some who thought it was built to hold the secret of the lost continent of Atlantis . . . if such a place ever existed. One tale said the stones had been brought to Salisbury from Africa by giants! And a later tale said Merlin brought them himself from Wales in a whirlwind!

In the 18th and 19th century, it became fashionable for famous artists to paint the site of Stonehenge. Many showed it as a peaceful country scene with people on picnics and children and animals scampering around the stones. However, the land surrounding Stonehenge was never farmed.

It doesn't seem likely that Stonehenge was built just to keep the people busy doing something. Nor does it appear to be a work of art put up to brighten the landscape. And even though the barrows did hold human bones, it was not simply a cemetery.

Stonehenge has been a place of mystery for hundreds of years.

Through Dr. Hawkins' work, we know that Stonehenge is some type of ancient computer or calculator. Stonehenge is not the only ancient structure in western Europe. At Avebury, twenty miles (32 km) north of Stonehenge, is another structure of giant stones. Avebury is probably several hundred years older than Stonehenge. The stones used here are in a much rougher, or natural, condition. They have not been smoothed the way the stones were at Stonehenge. The people of Avebury were probably the ancestors of the

*At Avebury, a circle of rough stones is surrounded by a very deep
ditch. Today, a highway runs through the site.*

people at Stonehenge. Avebury may have been too near the dense forests of the area for the land to be cultivated. So the people moved to the more open area near Salisbury Plain.

In northern England, in a place called Keswick Carles, there are thirty-nine stones from the early Bronze Age sitting in a circle. In western England, in the district of Cornwall, is Lanyon Quoit. This is one

This is New Grange, an ancient chambered tomb in Ireland.

of the most incredible examples of early English megaliths. Megaliths are stones that have not been dressed at all. They are simply rough stones, used as they were found. Lanyon Quoit is a barrow or burial mound. Several hundred years ago, three of the upright stones still stood. They were so high that a person on horseback could ride under the top capstone (lintel) without ducking his head. But in 1815 A.D., a violent

The entrance to the New Grange tomb has recently been restored.

storm leveled the stones. They were later re-erected, but not in their original form.

In Ireland and along the west coast of England, there are many ancient chamber tombs, some of them as many

42

as four thousand years old. In southern Brittany, a province in France, there are several thousand megaliths in an area called Carnac. Carnac also has several well-preserved barrows with rooms and underground chambers. It is known that the province of Brittany was originally settled by people from Cornwall in England. But we don't know if this is the reason for the similarity in the arrangement of the giant stones.

We probably shall never have all the answers to the

Although many answers to the Stonehenge mystery have been uncovered, many questions remain.

riddles of Stonehenge. Without a written history, an answer is impossible. But we are learning more all the time. With our modern scientific tools, such as carbon dating and computers, we have a better understanding of the people of Stonehenge.

Map

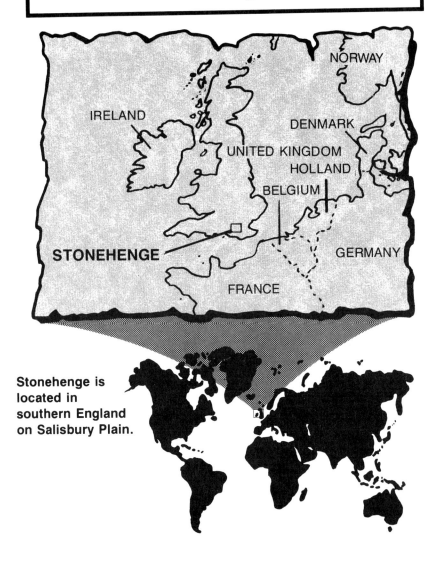

IRELAND

NORWAY

DENMARK

UNITED KINGDOM

HOLLAND

BELGIUM

STONEHENGE

GERMANY

FRANCE

Stonehenge is
located in
southern England
on Salisbury Plain.

Glossary/Index

ARCHAEOLOGIST 6, 9, 11, 17, 23, 33 — *A scientist who studies the remains of past human life.*

ARCHITECT 19 — *Someone who designs buildings.*

ASTRONOMICAL 7, 8, 33 — *Relating to the heavenly bodies, such as stars, planets, and galaxies.*

ASTROPHYSICIST 7 — *An astronomer who studies the physical and chemical makeup of the heavenly bodies.*

AXIS 6 — *A straight line around which an object turns or may be imagined to turn. The earth's axis passes through the North and South Poles.*

BARROWS 18, 36, 43 — *Burial holes.*

BRONZE AGE 12 — *The period in human culture characterized by the use of bronze tools. It began in Europe about 3500 B.C. and somewhat earlier in western Asia and Egypt.*

CARBON DATING 45 — *To establish the age of objects by measuring the amount of*

radioactive carbon remaining in them. This technique is often used by archaeologists.

CHAMBER TOMB 42 — *A building or room for dead bodies.*

CELTS 16, 17 — *Ancient tribes of the British Isles and western France.*

DRUIDS 4, 16, 17 — *The judges and priests of the Celtic tribes.*

HENGE 33 — *A 'hanging' or a 'gallows cross.'*

LINTEL 14, 30, 31, 32, 33, 41— *A flat piece above an opening, joining the two sides to form a 'doorway.'*

MAMMOTH 23 — *Very large; huge.*

MEGALITH 41, 43 — *A natural stone used in prehistoric monuments.*

PREHISTORIC 5 — *Of a time before events were written down.*

TENON and MORTISE 30, 31, 33 — *A projection (tenon) and a hole or groove (mortise) that together form a joint (union).*

47